red
like
fruit

also by hannah moscovitch

Bunny
The Children's Republic
East of Berlin
Fall On Your Knees (co-created with Alisa Palmer)
Infinity (with Njo Kong Kie)
Little One and Other Plays
Post-Democracy
The Russian Play and Other Short Works
Secret Life of a Mother (with Maev Beaty and Ann-Marie Kerr)
Sexual Misconduct of the Middle Classes
This Is War
What a Young Wife Ought to Know

"A true masterpiece."
—Dominic Corr, *Corr Blimey*

"An expert forensic search into the most ungraspable truths of womanhood."
—Divine Angubua, NEXT *Magazine*

"Written by Hannah Moscovitch, and the finalist for the Susan Smith Blackburn Prize, this super-smart and devastating two-hander is both formally and narratively galvanising . . . *Red Like Fruit* is slippery stuff, playing with ideas around consent and probing how we hear women's stories. In the process, it does something remarkable; it gives us all the voice to tell about the things we feel that nobody wants to hear . . . A supreme piece of acting."
—Lyn Gardner, *The Stage*

"Moscovitch's words shine through with a magnificent clarity, searching and searching again for some kind of truth among the overheated culture wars of our time."
—Joyce McMillan, *The Scotsman*

"Director Christian Barry gives the reverberating material the glass sharp, perfectly wrought and superbly acted production it demands."
—Mark Brown, *The National* (Scotland)

"This script is the spiky, incisive, brilliant love child of #MeToo . . . but it never feels didactic. Instead, it feels like the story of every twenty-first century Western woman has finally, magnificently, been transported to the stage. Beware: it might make you weep with rage."
—Claire Wood, *The Wee Review*

"Vivid, topical and beautifully written, the acting superlative. Top marks all round."
—Greg Holstead, *North West End* UK

red
like
fruit

hannah
moscovitch

playwrights canada press
toronto

Red Like Fruit © 2025 by Hannah Moscovitch
First edition: October 2025
Printed and bound in Canada by Imprimerie Gauvin Ltée, Gatineau

Cover design by Monnet Design
Author photo by Alejandro Santiago

Playwrights Canada Press
202-269 Richmond St. W., Toronto, ON M5V 1X1
416.703.0013 | info@playwrightscanada.com | www.playwrightscanada.com

For professional or amateur production rights, please contact:
Colin Rivers, Marquis Literary
www.mqlit.ca | colin@mqent.ca

LIBRARY AND ARCHIVES CANADA CATALOGUING IN PUBLICATION
Title: Red like fruit / Hannah Moscovitch.
Names: Moscovitch, Hannah, author
Description: First edition.
Identifiers: Canadiana (print) 20250175436 | Canadiana (ebook) 20250175444
   | ISBN 9780369105646 (softcover) | ISBN 9780369105653 (PDF)
   | ISBN 9780369105660 (EPUB)
Subjects: LCGFT: Drama.
Classification: LCC PS8626.O837 R43 2025 | DDC C812/.6—dc23

Playwrights Canada Press staff work across Turtle Island, on Treaty 13 and Treaty 20 territories, as well as unceded lands, which are the current, ancestral, and future homes of the Anishinaabe Nations (Ojibwe / Chippewa, Odawa, Potawatomi, Algonquin, Saulteaux, Nipissing, and Mississauga / Michi Saagiig), the Wendat, members of the Haudenosaunee Confederacy (Mohawk, Oneida, Onondaga, Cayuga, Seneca, and Tuscarora), and the xʷməθkʷəẏəm (Musqueam), Sḵwx̱wú7mesh (Squamish), and səlilwətaɬ (Tsleil-Waututh) Nations, as well as Metis and Inuit peoples. It always was and always will be Indigenous land.

We acknowledge the financial support of the Canada Council for the Arts, the Ontario Arts Council (OAC), Ontario Creates, the Government of Ontario, and the Government of Canada for our publishing activities.

to Christian Barry

Red Like Fruit was first produced by 2b theatre company at the Bus Stop Theatre, Halifax, from April 3 to 21, 2024, with the following cast and creative team:

Lauren: Michelle Monteith
Luke: David Patrick Flemming

Director: Christian Barry
Designer: Kaitlin Hickey
Stage Manager: Don Brownrigg
Production Manager: Sylvia Bell
Accessibility Coordinator: Sara Graham

characters

Lauren (in her early forties)
Luke

notes

What Lauren is doing while Luke speaks is up to the director. It could
be abstract. It could be choreography. It could be some version of
nothing. Lauren, though, listens to Luke and watches the audience.
That's her main thing. Luke's main thing is inhabiting Lauren's voice.

running time

An hour and fifteen minutes.

prologue

LAUREN: Hi.
I'm Lauren.
This is Luke.

LUKE: Hi.

LAUREN: I've asked Luke to speak for me.

> *LAUREN sits and LUKE remains standing.*
> *LUKE looks at LAUREN.*

LUKE: *(to LAUREN)* Yeah?

LAUREN: *(to LUKE)* Yeah.

LUKE: Okay.
Let's start.

> *Shift.*

Start.

LUKE: Lauren buys a coffee
Crosses the street
And goes into CAMH
Which is
A mental hospital
In Toronto.
She goes down the long corridor
Finds the room
Looks around at the other women and feels deeply, deeply uncool.
She thinks mostly it's women who do this in groups
Isn't it?
Talk about their problems?
Their Daddy hang-ups
Their shitty exes
And how they can't move on.
Men click on porn
Go fishing
Get loaded
Cry into each other's shirts
Pretend they didn't?
The session hasn't started so Lauren spends the first few minutes
trying to solve shit on her phone
Set up interviews for an article she's been assigned (a high-profile
case of domestic violence)
Which counteracts her feeling of uncoolness and distracts her from

The drab room and the overweight women.
The psychologist comes in
And Lauren wonders if he can
Help her?
He explains the hopes and anticipated outcomes and how untwist-
ing your thinking is the optimal whatever.
The psychologist
Asks them each to say why they're in group.
There's a thoughtful silence.
Lauren is surprised
She finds she likes
That none of the women laugh or roll their eyes.
One of them
A woman named Alice
Says that after her husband left her
She regretted keeping the house so cold
Maybe if she'd kept it two degrees warmer he would've stayed and
not had sex with his assistant curator.
Lauren looks at the floor.
She can't help but think
But what if some men do just want a woman who's
A pretty object to have in the room
And companionship only comes when he's with other businessmen?
What in the end is the point of getting angry about that if that's what
some men want?
Then Alice the woman left by her husband
Says cautiously
That she doesn't think it was the temperature of her house.
Not really.
All along the problem was that her husband wanted a woman to
look up to him
Instead of one who looked directly at him
Which makes Lauren like Alice
Because she says it thoughtfully and without self-pity.
When it's Lauren's turn she says
"I'm not sure what's wrong with me."

Beat.

Half of Lauren's friends have a kid with autism or cerebral palsy or
They have nothing in their bank accounts in case of cancer.
Her husband's good
Her children are good
She has
Disposable income.
Aren't those all the preconditions for joy?
There isn't anything obviously wrong with her other than this vague
sense of
Unease
That's been escalating over the last few months.
The women look at her
Thinking through what she's said.
Lauren likes this too
That they're considering her attentively.
One of them says
"There might be things that don't make sense but that are real."
And another woman says
"It's okay if it's small things that have piled up into a big pile."
And that's when the psychologist intervenes
"I want to remind you all not to offer advice."
And Lauren
Who has been appreciating the advice
Thinks
"Huh."
"Huh."
"I'm angry."
And
"Maybe I should tell someone I get angry and I don't know why."
And anyway why be angry?
This psychologist's probably right that advice from these women
who aren't professionals could be unhelpful.

Shift.

When the session ends
Lauren goes home
Kisses her husband
(He's on his way to pick up a client from the airport and take them
to a baseball game to "build rapport.")
Sits down in her home office
To work on the article about domestic violence.
An employee
Of the Liberal Party
In a top position
Was charged with assaulting his long-term girlfriend.
He pled guilty and was sentenced to community work
And then he'd been rehired at his old job
And somehow it was all hushed up and is only now hitting the news
Which seems almost impossible
Like how did this slip through the cracks?
The man's name is *Andrew*
Lauren thinks.
It feels improbable that anyone named Andrew who has a good
track record on climate change beats his wife.

Shift.

Lauren calls Andrew's boss
Justin the MP.
When the phone picks up
The man on the line says
"Is this about the slap?"
And Lauren thinks
"Oh okay"
"A slap."
She has no problem imagining herself losing her temper and want-
ing to if not going through with a slap.
As they make pleasant opening comments Justin sounds
Assured.
That steady authority of a man who has been listened to often

Friendly enough within the parameters of a political operative.
Lauren asks
Neutrally
How Justin became aware of the incident?
Justin says Andrew came into the office the next day pale and "off"
and told him there had been a bad situation with Brittany.
Only later did Justin understand police were involved
That it was a criminal matter.
Justin's answer sounds rehearsed
A more polished version of the truth arrived at through repetition
and that's fine
Lauren expected that.
Lauren asks
"And what were Andrew and Brittany like to work with?"
And here Justin hesitates.
She hears his mental manoeuvring.
Lauren takes her hands off her laptop keys and waits.
When Justin speaks
His tone suggests that
It's uncomfortable to be in a position of conveying an unsavoury
truth that doesn't align with his political values.
Justin says
"Brittany had a tendency toward attention-seeking behaviour."
She had
As far as he knows
Reasons for her behavioural issues
And here there's an implication that there are traumas in Brittany's
childhood that can't be mentioned or that the whole of Brittany's
childhood was a trauma
And it's horrible to say
And no one wants it to be the case
But that is how Brittany was.
There's also a slight implication in Justin's tone that Andrew is one of
these men who picks vacuous volatile women.
There's a pause and then
Lauren asks

"Andrew hit her?"
Justin doesn't hesitate at all now.
Yes
Andrew slapped her.
He did
Yes.
Lauren says mildly
I have two children
I tell them "don't hit."
Lauren can sense that Justin smiles indulgently.
He says
"Yes, agreed."
"Andrew shouldn't have hit her."
But there's something in his tone that suggests Justin would have
liked to hit Brittany himself
And that Brittany almost wanted to be hit so she could garner the
sympathy or attention or attention in the form of sympathy she was
so desperate for.
And also something in Justin's tone
That suggests that of course Brittany is going to do what Brittanies
in these circumstances do
Which is make herself the centre of attention
And Brittany is both dangerous and pitiable.
Lauren asks
"You hired Andrew back?"
On the other end of the line Justin seems to be nodding.
Justin's tone has an apology in it
Yes it would've been better for them not to rehire Andrew from an
ethical and also an optical standpoint
But Andrew's work as an organizer within the party is critical
And Andrew had gone through the judicial process and been penal-
ized and rehabilitated and it was the hope of the Liberal Party that
the Canadian judicial system works.
Lauren asks
"And where is Brittany employed now?"
And here there's an intake of breath

And a rueful tone that implies that
Yes
Lauren has done her job and caught Justin out.
Yes.
"Good point."
Yes
Brittany's role was less senior and her contract wasn't renewed.
At this juncture in the interview Justin pauses and tells Lauren he
read a couple of her articles ahead of this interview and she's a very
good journalist.
The implication is that Justin knows or trusts that Lauren won't
stoop to sensationalism.
His voice is steady
Confident.
The compliment rings true.
And this Lauren supposes is
Charm?
The call concludes with Justin calmly offering further help.
Yes they want to be transparent with her
And yes they knew the media might have
And here his tone implies
"Very valid" questions about why they are continuing to employ
Andrew.
Lauren nods and nods and then hangs up the phone.
She sits at her desk
Head tilted to one side.
Lauren realizes she wanted Justin to like her
Which is
Unsettling.

    Beat.

Then Lauren rouses herself and dials this woman who was slapped
by her ex-boyfriend.
The phone rings a number of times before the woman picks up.
She sounds

Neutral on the phone
Cautious.
Lauren asks her what happened.
The woman
Named Brittany
Which somehow doesn't help her case
Says
"I lost two teeth."
And then
"He was on top of me
Punching me
And yeah part of
Part of what
What happened was that after he punched me like that he had uh
Sex
Intercourse with me and I wasn't saying no to the sex exactly but my
teeth had been pushed back against the roof of my mouth."
Lauren at her laptop blinks
Closes her eyes
Clears her throat
Asks
What Brittany thinks about Andrew's version of the story
That it was a slap.
Brittany says quietly
"I don't have any thoughts about that."
But in Brittany's tone Lauren hears wariness and something else
Is it confusion?
Or tamped-down rage?
Or exhaustion?
A desire to gently put the phone down and walk away?
Lauren asks
"What do you think about Andrew being hired back at his
former job?"
Brittany says
"I don't feel great about it."
Lauren asks

"What do you think about them not hiring you back?"
Brittany says mildly
"I wouldn't have gone back anyway."
Lauren asks
"Had Andrew ever hit you in the past?"
Brittany says
"Not—no . . . "
Lauren waits
Lets a pause open up.
Brittany says
"He shoved me during arguments a couple of times."
Lauren asks
Formally
If she can call back with any further questions that might arise.
Brittany says "yes" but there's a sense
As they hang up
That Brittany's hoping not to hear from her again.
And this
Here is where
It doesn't make sense
And Lauren doesn't know why
Aside from the obvious.
The incident Brittany described is disturbing.
(But she's covered worse.)
The uneasiness she's tried to describe to various doctors in various
clinical settings sets in.
This feeling of constriction
Of
As though
She's
Being dragged backward
Toward some
Horrible

> LAUREN *closes her eyes for a moment.*
> LUKE *turns and regards her.*

To diffuse the feeling
Lauren goes on Twitter and clicks and clicks.

LUKE glances at LAUREN *again. Her eyes are still closed.*

I'm sorry.
Are
Are you okay?

LAUREN opens her eyes.

LAUREN: Oh yeah.
Yeah
Fine.

LUKE: Okay.
Sorry.

Beat.

I'll
Go back to the . . . ?

LAUREN: Yeah.

LUKE returns to the text.

LUKE: Next Lauren gets on the phone with the ex-boyfriend himself
Andrew
And asks for his comment.
She keeps her voice jokey and low
To make herself sound more like a buddy of his.
Andrew says
"I did the wrong thing.
I did
I was charged and I pled guilty.

Now I'm trying to put my life back together."
He sounds so impossibly normal and reasonable
Like a person who made a singular mistake.
Lauren asks him
"How do you feel about Brittany's injuries?"
Andrew says he slapped her while she was balanced on a chair in
their kitchen and she lost her balance and
She fell backward into a wall.
Lauren asks how it happened.
Andrew pauses and says
"If you've read the police report . . .
Britanny was drunk."
When Lauren asks about punching he says "no"
He slapped her
Open-handed
One time
No punching.
Lauren says
"What about the teeth that were bent back against the roof of
Brittany's mouth and the surgeries to remove those teeth and then
to replace those teeth first with dentures on a twenty-seven-year-
old woman and then the four or five surgeries for implants over the
course of twenty-one months?"
There's a pause
Then Andrew says quietly
"Yeah
It must have been terrible."
And
"I remember the sound when she hit the wall."
And then
"I watched her fall backward and immediately I knew how bad it
was going to be and and I remember how sick I felt that I had done
that to her."
And then
"It wasn't a good night."

They talk a little longer about the courses Andrew was required to
complete on how not to commit domestic violence and on the other
men he met along the way (here it sounds like Andrew made some
blue-collar friends) and his community service at a public library and
what it was like to return to his job with the Liberal Party and if he
was welcomed back or if there was any residual wariness or mistrust
(yes many jokes were made in the style of "don't piss off Andrew").
At the end of the call Andrew says
"I know it'll sound self-serving
But I want you to know I lost it in that moment and I lashed out but
I didn't mean for her to sustain that kind of damage to her teeth I
really didn't and I've been trying to figure out why I did something
that was so obviously wrong and bad."
Then concluding pleasantries and
Lauren slowly puts down the phone.
She imagines her son as a grown man with the same half-smile as
her husband
And he's arguing with a girl
A blond girl who wears flip-flops and posts a lot of photos of herself
at the beach with captions like
"I am soooooo loaded."
Lauren pictures this girl saying some offhand stupid thing and then
her son
Smacks this girl.
The shocked look on her son's face as the girl stumbles and one knee
twists and touches the ground.
And the call she'd receive from her son
Emotion slurring his voice
"Mom, I lost it, I did something bad."
And isn't that
Is that
Is it okay to make a mistake?
How much good behaviour can we expect all the time from all the
Boys?
Men?

LAUREN exhales and leans forward, holding her head in her hands, her fingers in her hair. LUKE turns and looks at her momentarily.

Lauren
I'm sorry.
Are you good?

LAUREN: Good.

LAUREN, her head still down, nods.

Yeah.
Yes.
Just . . .
We're
Getting into it.

LUKE: Do you want to stop for a sec?

LAUREN: No.
Uh
No
But I am uh
Probably gonna uh
Along the way
It might be . . .

LUKE: Yeah
Of course.

LAUREN: It's okay.
You can keep going.

LUKE goes back to the text.

LUKE: Late that night
Lauren lies in bed beside her husband
Listening to the house
Hoping her thoughts will disarticulate into sleep.
The dryer down in the basement is squeaking
And out on the street streetcars are going by
And then
The grey corridors of her mind turn onto an unfamiliar street
Cobblestoned.
She thinks
"Oh it's
Is it
Prague?"
When she was fifteen?
A family holiday in Prague?
Her parents beside her on the cobblestoned street and Lauren bored
and sulky and annoyed to be spending so much time with her
family and her mother lecturing her about her "lack of gratitude"
and then her father hiring a tour guide to escort the family around a
semi-submerged crypt.
The tour guide with the big moustache who seemed so
warm-hearted.
Once they were down in the crypt
The tour guide was
Helping her to not trip in the darkened underground tunnels
On the uneven rocks
But as he'd helped he'd caught her
Between her legs.

   Beat.

And no joke her mother and father and little brother and little sister
were no more than ten feet ahead.
She'd tried to speed up in the darkened crypt and put her mother
and father between her and the moustached man and she'd fallen
and skinned her knee

And her father had said
"Lauren, come on. What are you doing? Don't run in the dark."
Out in the sunlight she watched the tour guide closely
But no he seemed professional and barely looked at her.
And then
Her mom had said in an upbraiding tone
"Lauren, thank the tour guide."
And Lauren had
Turned and
Thanked the tour guide
So as not to seem like she lacked gratitude.
What a weird thing to remember and with so little emotion attached
to it.
Lauren throws off the duvet and gets up.
She walks down the hallway to her daughter's and son's bedrooms
Stops in their doorways like she's in a movie to watch them sleep.
But unmovie-like she's thinking
What
In the end
Does it matter?
What
In the end
Is the difference between trauma and experience?
Because aren't those small *whatever* things that happen in adoles-
cence just a part of it all?

Beat.

Standing in the hallway outside—

LAUREN: Aren't . . .

LUKE looks at LAUREN.

Aren't those things just part of it all?
Aren't they?

Shift.

Sorry to interrupt and
Ask you
But
I can't help but think that.

LUKE: Part of what?

LAUREN: I don't know
Growing up?

LUKE: Uh
Well
Uh
I can try
To answer that.
You want me to?

LAUREN: Yeah.

LUKE: Okay uh
The tour guide
He was trying to stop you from tripping?

*LAUREN **nods.***

LAUREN: Yeah he was.

LUKE: And how did he do it?

LAUREN: As I tripped forward on the rocks
He caught me but he didn't put his hands on my waist:
He uh

LUKE: So you tripped forward and he caught you
But as he caught you
He caught you by the
So you trip and he catches you by the
Vagina?

    LAUREN nods.
    LUKE looks at *LAUREN*.

LAUREN: Okay yeah.

LUKE: I don't
I don't
I think there were better ways for him to stop you from tripping.
Don't you?
How could that have helped?
I don't mean to sound glib and I understand you're asking me a
broader question about growing up but I don't
I'm not sure how to
Answer the broader question?

LAUREN: No yeah.

LUKE: The simple answer is yeah
He was using it being dark and you being fifteen and you being
scared or embarrassed and staying quiet to
Put his hands on you.

    LAUREN gazes at him for a moment, trying to orient herself.

LAUREN: Yeah.

    Pause.

LUKE: I'll go on?

LAUREN: Yeah.

LUKE returns to the text.

LUKE: Standing in the hallway outside her children's rooms
Lauren turns
And goes into her home office.
She fumbles through her handbag
Finds her phone
Calls her dad on his cell.
He's usually up late in his office playing the stock market.
When he picks up and asks her what's going on
She says
"I don't know, Dad.
I'm fine I think?"
After a few minutes of small talk with her dad
(Apparently his stock portfolio is doing great!)
Lauren starts to cry.
It's soothing to listen to her dad's exhilaration over making money
while she cries silently
Because yes
She's pissed off that she's having these weird thoughts about her
childhood and what was okay and what wasn't
And yes
Her father
If he thought about it
Could surmise that if his daughter is calling this late at night then
maybe there's something wrong
But what's the point of
Wanting your father to notice something he isn't going to notice?
Lauren hangs up the phone and finds somehow hanging up makes it
worse and she puts her head down and cries
But why get
Worked up about it all?

Shift.

The next morning
Once the children have been driven to school and Lauren's walked
around the house picking up
The small shirts the breakfast bowls the glittery pieces of confetti all
over the floor from an art project
She sits back down at her laptop
Tries to still herself.
Her first interview is with a neighbour of Brittany and Andrew's
that she's gotten in touch with by painstakingly reading through the
police report
And now
An elderly woman comes on the phone
Named Gladys.

LAUREN looks up leaning forward on her elbows.

Lauren says
"Thank you for your time."
And Gladys says
"Of course, dear."
Lauren says
"You heard the fight that night?"
Gladys says yes
Through the walls
Thumping and wailing and
Brittany saying "let me up" a number of times . . .
Gladys pauses then and says
"The sound of it wasn't right, like a child or a dog crying."
Lauren feels herself sit upright
And lean forward.
She asks what Gladys's impressions were of Andrew.
Gladys says
"Oh him?
He's a stone-cold creep."
And Lauren
Blinks

And blinks
And says
"You didn't say that to the police."
And Gladys says no
They asked her questions about what happened
They didn't ask her to characterize either Brittany or Andrew.
And immediately Lauren realizes how stupid she sounds
As though she hasn't covered cases like this one before
Of course you don't characterize
You just answer the questions the police ask you.

Shift.

The next call is to the ER resident who saw Brittany that night.
His name is Doctor Daniel Kim and he gets on a Zoom call from his
office at the hospital.
Right away Lauren thinks he has a good professional manner.
Even though he looks young there's something about him that
strikes her as impartial.
Doctor Kim tells her in a curt tone that he advised Brittany not to
waive her doctor-patient confidentiality for a magazine article.
The implication being that Brittany is too vulnerable—or possibly
too reckless?—to look after herself.
Lauren goes over what Andrew told her about the incident.
Doctor Kim listens to her carefully
Impassively
Then he tells her without hesitation that when he saw Brittany
She looked like a car-accident victim
Because of the severity of the injuries
Teeth pushed back
Lacerations
And the amount of blood from the head wound.
Doctor Kim says Brittany was silent when she came in in the ambu-
lance accompanied by police
Silent but conscious.
He found that worrying.

Lauren at that moment catches sight of herself in the Zoom window
and sees she's grimacing.
Lauren asks if the type of abrasions on Brittany's face and arms were
consistent with a slap and falling into a wall?
Doctor Kim considers the question cooly then says that he doesn't
have the expertise to assess that.
That would be a question for the police.
Lauren asks if there's anything Doctor Kim would like to add.
He thinks for a moment
Looking down
Then he says
"Yeah I'd like to add: don't beat up women."

Shift.

The detachment Lauren feels turns into
Something
Else that is
So big and pit-like.

LAUREN *looks down.*
Shift.

Lauren dials the number for her final interview of the day
With Brittany's mother
Who
Sounds sensible
No-nonsense
If a little reluctant to speak about "this whole thing" again.
The mother
Whose name is Judy
And who works as an administrator at a hospital
Says
Brittany is
Her daughter of course
But

Brittany has had a tendency that they all hoped she'd grow out of
toward
Not lying but exaggeration
And that Brittany "is a drinker" and a bit of a "chaos agent"
And yes of course Andrew hit her
Which makes him a jackass
But somehow Brittany
Is very good at "playing the victim" when the need arises.
Brittany was diagnosed with borderline personality disorder
And Judy wouldn't be surprised if these type of things keep happen-
ing in her daughter's life.
Judy admits to Lauren
She'd liked Andrew
Because he seemed so stable until
What happened happened.
Lauren asks carefully about what Brittany's childhood was like
And
Judy says
"I have two daughters and one of them is just fine
And the other one is
Brittany."
And after more of this
Of Judy's brittle admissions that there's something wrong with her
daughter
Lauren hangs up the phone and closes the lid of her laptop.
She gets up stiffly
Thinks to herself
"That's enough
I can't think about this anymore."

LAUREN *takes out a tube of lipstick and applies it.*

She finds a tube of lipstick
Smears it on
A bright
Orange-red

Checks her emails on her phone to make sure her children are okay
Grabs her handbag
And heads out.
A lunch with a colleague.

Shift.

The restaurant is a good one and she's looking forward to the quality
of the food
The quality of the conversation she'll have with this colleague.
The colleague is a couple of minutes late.
Lauren orders a glass of wine
And enjoys the thoughts that flick through her mind.
That it's good to be her age.
The age where you can sit in a restaurant by yourself
Sipping a glass of wine
Looking out at the world
Blunted
With a sense of humour about it all.
The confusion of being young and having no clear love
No clear career
No clear life turned down.
Lauren's colleague shows up.
As he takes off his coat and scarf he's already talking about the pall
that's fallen in the wake of the MeToo Movement
Over the journalism department where he's an associate professor.
He tells her in quick broken phrases
That he's
(The waitress takes their order but it doesn't break his flow.)
He's thinking about the men he knows
And speculating about which of them
If any
Like to get their dick out at work
Corner women in their offices
Hit on them when all the cues point to "fuck off."
These men

Who must somehow conclude that a woman
Blond
An intern
Or a student
Only twenty-one years old
Could be very hot for a man with greying hair and a puffy gut and
diminishing sex appeal.
While Lauren sips her white wine
Lauren's colleague is saying
That he's not sure he gets on an animal level
What the whole "getting your dick out to just show it to someone" is
all about
Or putting your phone down your pants and clicking.
What's the gratification of knowing your dick is out there on some-
one else's phone?
Just dick in the wind
But all around him men are falling like suicides off buildings so
there must be a set of unsavoury predilections that he's personally
unfamiliar with or hopes he is.
Lauren looks at her colleague
And his mouth moving and moving.
She could say to him
Yes she too feels unsettled these days
She too feels as though the world's tilted sideways
But instead she listens
And listens
Until
In her mind
A bathtub
A bathtub filled with blood

Shift.

Lauren's colleague's still going on and on with obvious personal discomfort about the MeToo Movement.
It crosses Lauren's mind that

In all this time of her colleague monologuing
In forty-five minutes of him monologuing and her unhuhing it
hasn't occurred to him that she is
A woman and might have
Thoughts
About the MeToo Movement.
And with that thought comes fucked-up feelings
And sudden-onset rage
Like she'd like to punch her colleague in the mouth
This long-time friend of hers who's been to her house many times
for dinner parties
Who she's shared so much of her life
Her career with
Who was there cooing at her son three days after his birth
And
Maybe it's the midday wine
Or a sudden inner capitulation
She looks down at the spoils of their lunch
And up at her colleague and the restaurant behind him
At the streetscape beyond
And life happening
And finally her colleague says
"Oh fuck."
And "Oh no."
And "Why are you crying?"
And Lauren has to smile and wipe tears away quickly and make
something up.

  Shift.

When Lauren gets home she drops her bag and coat in the front
hallway and sits down in her home office.
She lifts the top of her laptop
And she opens the Andrew-Brittany audio files
And then she sees herself
At seventeen years old

Wandering the airport in Delaware
A distant cousin
Second or third but still for various reasons
Friendships within the family
This cousin was close with her aunt and her mother
And all of the joint family members think it's so kind that he's taking
an interest in his young cousin.
Lauren's cousin
Dean
Had offered to have her come and stay for a couple of days with
him in
Delaware
So they could have what was in those days called "quality time"
together.
Dean was in his thirties
An engineer
Owned a small landscaping business
Which
At the time
Lauren childishly thought involved clipping shrubs into shapes
But in fact involved cement trucks
And Dean
Sitting in an office in a managerial role
Hiring
Overseeing.
And that night when Lauren had showed up at the small Delaware
airport
He'd been standing with a big sign that read
Cousin Lauren.
When he'd seen her he'd grinned and hugged her
And he'd given her
Lollipops
As a joke?
Or?
She'd unwrapped one

In his car on the drive from the airport
And yes and this was
He'd glanced over at her a few times while he was driving.
She could remember a sense of his amusement but also
Interest in her
And she knew?
Did she know what sucking on a lollipop might mean to him?
And of looking sideways at him while she did it?
During the car ride they'd talked about Dean's health because
Dean had had bladder cancer the previous year.
All the background family chatter all year had been about him
His chemo
His mood
The prognosis for bladder cancer
Schedules of those family members in Delaware
Who was going with him to chemo
Who was sitting with him as he threw up
Who was making his meals
Who was feeding his dog.
Dean
Was attractive
A little hollowed out by the cancer but that square-jawed
American handsomeness.
They'd gone to a bar that night
Her small suitcase in the trunk of his car
And he'd bought her drinks
Which at seventeen felt adult
To be at a bar with a pint in front of her.
Not the drinking itself
She'd drunk a lot at house parties
But to be sitting and talking over beers
Men playing darts in the background.
Later that night
She'd brushed her teeth in Dean's bathroom
Smearing toothpaste on her toothbrush drunkenly

Then she'd fallen asleep in the spare bed.
In the middle of the night she'd woken up and as she woke up she
understood that
That what was waking her up was
Dean
On top of her body
Kissing her
And
Once she understood it was real
She was able to unclench her body
Which felt rigid and Dean
Was murmuring things to her
That her lips were
So red
Like fruit
That there was a quality to her skin
That
Made him know
He was on the other side of cancer
How he felt more than ever now he had to grab ahold of things,
of life
And as they kissed and fumbled he told her he loved her
And
Here she
Did he mean as her cousin?
Could he mean the other . . . ?
Or both in some way she couldn't?
That wasn't accounted for in how she
Thought about
Love?
And all through this Dean seemed as though this is normal
An anticipated outcome of Lauren coming to his house
Like of course this is what should be happening now and
Maybe because Dean seems so normal
And is acting like this is normal
And his voice is normal and he laughs in his normal way

She finds she is able to say to him
"No, not sex, I can't, I have my period."
And all through she keeps thinking
"I'm sure he thinks this is fine."
"I'm sure he can't tell."
Because while all this is happening she is so grossed out
By his cancer scar and by how hairy he is compared to the boys she's
used to
By how adult even his desires seem as he shows her how to give
him head
There is no embarrassment at talking her through what to do
And he's so confident as though this is routine for him to be doing
something sexual when for the boys she knows sexuality is still
more defined by newness than it is by pleasure
And the bodies of the boys are smooth and skinny and hairless and
something frightens her about Dean's body
Its roughness
It doesn't smell like the boys she knows
Like sample cologne
It smells like sweet sweat
And for Lauren there is no sexuality in this.
She is not turned on but only too alert
As though she is painfully trying not to let him know how sickened
she is
And she can't work out why she can't stop it
She cannot work out how to say no.
She does not once
Not once
Say no.
She doesn't say no.
She doesn't.
And by now it's light outside
And there are almost no thoughts in her head because
To have a thought would be too
And Dean smiles down at her
And gets out of bed to run her a bath.

LAUREN *wipes her lipstick off.*

As soon as Dean leaves her alone in the bathroom she takes out
her tampon
Drops it in the toilet
It's so heavy with blood it makes a wet thud
And then she gets right in the bath.
Long minutes she sits there
Head down in silence.
As the bathtub fills up with blood
She is thinking:
This is terrible.
This
Is terrible
Because soon I'm going to
Go
Out of this room and into the house and into the world and how am
I going to do that?

Shift.

An hour later
Dean drove her to her aunt's house
And Lauren had breakfast with him and her aunt.
Lauren remembers looking down at the eggs and toast and thinking
how weird it was that they were all sitting having breakfast like a family.
It felt like she couldn't get hold of
What had even
Happened in
Reality.
It was almost as though nothing *had happened.*
It seemed so improbable.
Sitting there joking and laughing with Dean and her aunt all the
normal ways conversations flowed
Which family dogs had died
Who had got into what colleges

And then a sudden upward glimpse of Dean's torso
His head thrown back
His hands in her hair
And then
"Was she looking forward to her last year of high school?"
She felt almost as though for the last twelve hours she'd been cold
and warmth was returning to her and breakfast was happening in a
hyperreal granular way
The taste of the eggs
The taste of the juice.
Dean and her aunt both had coffee.
She wasn't offered coffee because she was seventeen years old.
She drank her juice
And a few years later she told a college friend.
She downplayed it probably and the college friend laughed and said
"Oh fuck
The things that happen in your teens"
And rolled her eyes
And Lauren thinks, "Yes"
"Okay"
"Good"
"That's what I thought."
And she doesn't talk about it again for another fifteen years.

> *LAUREN gets up and walks around to the back of her chair.*
> *LUKE turns and looks at LAUREN.*
> *Who is standing somewhere on stage. He's again checking*
> *with her.*

LAUREN: I'm just not sure what
What to
Yeah
No
Sorry
I'm sorry
Go on.

LUKE: Yeah?

LAUREN: Yeah
I'm about to ask the question that's already in what I wrote.
I'm yeah
Getting ahead of myself.
Sorry.

LUKE: Of course.
No problem.

LUKE returns to the text.

In college
When Lauren'd lived in that place in Montreal that was so romantic
A walk-up apartment with high vaulted ceilings in that style that
was so cheap and so plentiful in Montreal back then
And that boyfriend
Who wasn't a boyfriend yet
Just a crush
Somehow
He'd figured out she had a crush on him
And on a school trip
To New York City to the opera
They'd sat on the Greyhound bus
Glancing at each other every few minutes.
The Greyhound had pulled up at a gas station for a pit stop
And he'd
Taken her by the hand
Walked her behind the gas station and the fast-food joints
To a bank of pay phones
Pushed her body against it
His knee between her legs
Kissed her as hard as he could
While classmates
Came and went getting Tim Hortons in the background.

And then he'd let go of her and they'd rejoined the throng
And she'd gotten back on the bus
And sat down
Beside some girl who also liked opera
The bus jolting her
And jolting her
And Lauren had to
Breathe so as not to cum.
And back in Montreal
He'd found her on campus
Asked himself over
And they'd drunk the wine they could afford from the local
depanneur
And they'd fucked
And
Fallen asleep
And she'd woken up at 2 a.m. to
Him
On top of her
Kissing her
Pushing her legs open
And
Half-in and out of sleep they'd fucked like that four times
And each time
She'd woken up at some point before the sex but not long before
the sex.
With him
She'd liked that
And what in the end was the difference?
And also
How is it different than that time
She got drunk and
Did a couple of bumps of coke
And it seemed like a good idea
To fuck the
Sous chef

At the restaurant where she was working
And
She
Took him home
And as soon as he was inside her
Even as
They were still fucking
Even as it felt good
She regretted it and felt the beginnings of self-disgust.
Because the sous chef was
Only moderately attractive
And as he talked to her while fucking her she knew he was not a
very interesting person
And she'd
Because of the coke
And the good lighting at the restaurant
Miscalculated
And now she
Wanted him gone
Out of her body
Out of her room
And wasn't that
Isn't that?
What in the end is the difference between that sous chef and her
cousin?
The worst of it was she had sex she didn't want or regretted
Or what do you call sex that you are regretting as you are having it?
All you can do is think to yourself
As cheerfully as you can
Well that was terrible!
And move on.

*LAUREN moves toward LUKE and stands near him, as if about
to ask a question.*
LUKE turns and looks at LAUREN.

LAUREN: I mean
Yeah
That's my question.
What's the difference?

LUKE: Uh
The difference between your cousin and the sous chef?

LAUREN: Yeah.

LUKE: Uh
Okay
Yeah I can
Okay.
I can try to answer that.

> *Beat.*
> *LUKE considers.*

Okay well so with your cousin
He comes into the spare bedroom where you're staying at his house
in the middle of the night?

LAUREN: Yeah.

LUKE: And what's he wearing?

LAUREN: He's not wearing anything.

> *Beat.*

LUKE: He
He comes into your room naked?

LAUREN: I mean I don't know because I don't know where he took
his clothes off—

LUKE: But when you woke up he wasn't wearing any?

LAUREN: No.

LUKE: Okay.
Okay so
While you were asleep he got undressed
And then for a while he was on top of you touching you before you
woke up?

LAUREN: I don't think that long—

LUKE: And—okay—
And when you woke up was he turned on?

LAUREN looks at LUKE.

He was?

LAUREN looks away.

Okay cool
Cool.

Beat.

I think it's pretty clear what happened.
And I think it's clear why it's different for your cousin who shouldn't
a) fuck his cousin and b) fuck his much younger cousin and c) come
into his much younger cousin's bed in the middle of the night and
start having sex with her while she's not awake so that by the time
she wakes up he's jumped over the whole part where she can say yes
or no.
I don't think starting to have sex with someone—
Anyone
Especially a seventeen-year-old family member—

When they're not awake is
Okay?

    Beat.

And to answer your question yeah I think that's different than a
boyfriend who you already had sex with that night making an
assumption in the middle of the night that you might like more sex
with him.
And I don't think that's the same as the sous chef who you wanted to
have sex with at least until you didn't want to anymore because you
did at one point want to.
And with your cousin that wasn't the case.

LAUREN: But does he know it's different?

LUKE: Who?
Dean?

LAUREN: Especially because I didn't say no.

LUKE: Yeah
No
I think he knows.

LAUREN: But what was he thinking during all of that?
Wasn't he thinking
"I'm handsome
She's pretty
She ate those lollipops and she kept looking at me while she was
eating them
I'll teach her something about sex
I'm an attractive older man
She's going to have a nice time with me
She came to my house
She came to spend the night at my house

What did she think was going to happen?"
Something like that?

LUKE: Sure
Maybe
Whatever he was thinking
Whatever it was
He wasn't thinking about you.

Beat.

LAUREN: Yeah.

Beat.

Okay but
Isn't it true that
So many fucked-up things happen when you're a teenager?
I have so many.
There were these boys in the parking lot at 7-Eleven.
I was going to buy candy and they tried to pull my dress up
And like I had to
Run away from them.
I was maybe thirteen.
They had to be nineteen or twenty.
There are so many of those things that happened.
I mean isn't it just normal?

Beat.

LUKE: I
Yeah
I
What you're saying doesn't convince me it's normal.
It convinces me that a lot of fucked-up things happened to you?

LAUREN: Yeah but that's the problem
I just feel like if I got frustrated by every one of them
Sure it was bad or could have been better or shouldn't have
happened
Maybe that's true
But it feels in poor taste to go on and on about it . . .

LUKE: . . . I yeah . . .

LAUREN: . . . Like I'm trying to draw attention to myself
Like I want everyone to feel sorry for me . . .

LUKE: I mean
Maybe it's not that you want to talk about it all the time or draw
attention to yourself
Maybe you just don't want radio silence?

LAUREN: So it doesn't make you feel embarrassed when I talk
about this
Because you seem embarrassed.

LUKE: I am embarrassed but I don't know if
That matters?

LAUREN: It does matter because I don't want to go around making
people feel embarrassed all the time.
I have to live with myself.
And on top of which the whole thing's messy in my mind.
I can hold onto it for a little that it shouldn't have happened or it was
just on the wrong side of being okay or borderline something and
then that goes away
And even saying this out loud I know I sound
Weak or
Fucked up
Which is not who I am normally.

If you met me professionally I'd seem like a different person
I'd seem professional
And why struggle to articulate something that no one wants to
hear anyway
That makes me feel stupid and sound confused
And that I don't even think is
Or can't place as being definitively one thing or another—

LUKE: I mean okay
I mean look
Yes to all that except the last part.
Because
Having to endure sex with a family member isn't maybe the best
way to kick off a normal sex life.
And to figure out how to tell the difference between good sex and
bad sex and wrong sex.

> *LAUREN looks at him.*
> *Then looks away.*
> *Pause.*

LAUREN: Yeah.

> *Beat.*

Yeah.

LUKE: Should I
Should I keep going?

LAUREN: Yeah.

> *LUKE returns to the text.*

LUKE: Since that night with Dean
Lauren hasn't seen him.

He lives in Delaware
It's not that hard to avoid people who live in
Delaware.
Dean
Sometimes contacts her on social media.
She doesn't answer
Mostly because she's confused about what to say
She's confused by her own desire to
Pretend it
Didn't happen and to be his cousin and have her aunts be her aunts.
She doesn't want to mess up all that and for what?
So that every holiday will be terrible?
So that the family will be uncomfortable
Truly uncomfortable
So that rifts will form between her mother and her aunts?
She's
And this is
The worst of it
Scared that if she does
See Dean
She'll be happy to see him
Because
Didn't he also when she was a little girl
Take her to the fair and win a massive cheap teddy bear for her that
she treasured and that sat in the corner of her room for six or seven
years slowly losing its stuffing?
And that part of their
Life
Their relationship
Is as strong
As that one night
Not enough maybe to totally obliterate it but
He's her cousin.
She can't just
Pretend he isn't.

Beat.

The next day
Lauren winds her way down the long institutional corridors at
CAMH to sit with the group of women in the dingy room.
She
Sits
Listens to the women
Who
Have a new set of
Cautious observations about their poor circumstances.
This one
Is losing her looks and with them her confidence and how is she
going to convince anyone to enter into a romance with a faded
blond with self-loathing issues?
That one
Has a boss who's always got a tone of surprise when she does good
work and makes high-handed statements like
"This press release was actually very well executed, Alice?!"
And what does that mean for her promotion track?
Lauren
Listens to the therapist tell them how to combat their maladaptive
thinking
How not to catastrophize.
How things are not as bad as the women think they are.
At the end of the session
A couple of the women wander down the sidewalk together
In the dirt and the noise of Toronto
Still talking
Animated
And into a coffee shop.
Lauren sits with them
And enjoys their ironic and thoughtful advice.
She feels
As she listens

She slips in and out of feelings of intense liking for them intermixed
with disgust
Which
And then after a while the conversation swirls downward into the
depths and she
Finds herself talking about
At first laughing but then talking openly
About
Her cousin
Dean.

Beat.

The women look back at her
Without shame
Without pity
Without a sudden stiffening that can happen when you admit to
something uncomfortable like this
Without laughing it off.
No one tries to calibrate their reaction and say the right words
No one jokes to alleviate their discomfort
None of that.
They are
Considering her
Carefully
Quietly
Until the woman named Alice says
"I don't know what the category is for that
I think you get to choose
But
Here's what's familiar about what you said.
I do feel like there's a
Voice
The voice of
I don't know

All of us
And it's saying:
'Sh
It's fine.
Shhhhh
You're fine.
It'll be over in a minute
It'll be fine
Just get through it
It's not that big a deal
Shhhhhh.' "
And the other women from the group
Lean in a little
As if to say
Yes
That is how it is
That's how it is.
And then one of the women says so quietly it's almost not said
"I'm sorry."

> *Beat.*

Later Lauren sits at her desk
Typing up the story about Andrew and Brittany
Putting it into sentences and paragraphs.
Her phone rings
And it's a number that's probably
Because of the area code
Going to be someone who's connected to the Andrew and Brittany
article
When Lauren picks up she immediately recognizes the voice as
Brittany's.
Lauren goes still
Waits.
Brittany says

Cautiously
"Do you have a minute?"
And Lauren says
"Yes."
There's a pause on the line and then Brittany says
"I have one thing to add
Would it be okay to add it?"
And Lauren says
"Yes of course.
And Brittany says
"I should have admitted to you on the phone that I drink too much.
And that a lot of my memories from that night are blurry.
My lawyer told me not to say that.
But
I want you to know that I don't know what happened and I may not
be the best witness to my own story."
Lauren, who is sitting there
Rigid
Unclenches and nods and says
"Yes of course."
And "thank you."
And then Lauren finds her voice again and asks
"What do you think happened to you that night?"
And Brittany says
Very softly
"I don't
I just
I don't know."

Shift.

epilogue

LUKE ***turns to*** *LAUREN.*

LUKE: And that's it
That's all of it.

LAUREN ***nods.***

LAUREN: Yeah.

LAUREN ***exhales.***

Beat.
LAUREN ***turns to the audience.***

That's it.
That's the end.
So
Thank you.

LAUREN ***turns to*** *LUKE.*

Thank you
Luke.

LUKE: I uh
Yeah

Beat.

I have to admit
That uh
That I
That I'm
Before we go
Before they go
Can I ask you something?

LAUREN: Yeah.

LUKE: Why did you want me to say all this for you?
Why didn't you say it yourself?
I'm wondering it.
I think some of them might be wondering it too.

LUKE gestures to the audience.

I
To be honest
I think some of them might be uncomfortable about a man saying it
all for you
Although I also think some of them probably didn't notice that
there's anything to notice about me saying it for you . . .

Then LAUREN pauses, considers.

Maybe you don't know the answer . . .
Maybe you don't know what I'm asking . . .

LAUREN: Uh
No I do
Uh so because I'm a journalist I wrote it all down
And then lately I wanted to hear the whole thing in front of

LAUREN gestures to the audience.

People
And I wanted a voice that was
Neutral and steady
And had authority
That's believable
To tell it.
So that I could maybe better figure out what to think about it all.

LAUREN thinks about what she just said.
She swallows down emotion.

Which . . . ?
Yeah
I mean yeah.
I mean
Hunh.

Beat.

Does that . . . ?

LUKE: Yeah no that's clear
I get it uh
Yeah
And uh
How was that?

LAUREN considers him for as long as she wants.

LAUREN: Yeah
It was good.
It helped.
I feel

Clearer
Than I have
But uh
I guess
I guess
I could have been the one to tell it
Well
Doesn't matter
Does it?
I feel better.

>   *LAUREN considers LUKE.*
>   *LUKE considers LAUREN.*

LUKE: You feel better?

LAUREN: I do.
I feel better.

>   *Slowly, slowly, slowly LAUREN turns to the audience.*

It helped.
You
You helped.
Thank you.

>   *End play.*

acknowledgements

The author would like to thank Canada Council for the Arts, Dalhousie University, Soulpepper Theatre Company, Luminato Festival, and above all 2b theatre for the development of this work.

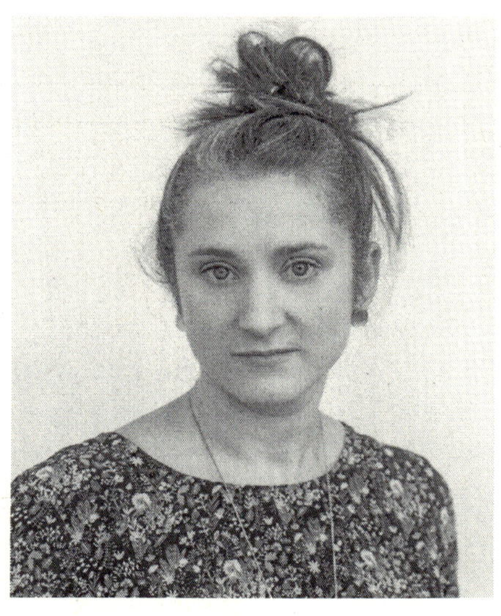

Hannah Moscovitch is one of Canada's most prominent playwrights. She has written sixteen plays, including *East of Berlin*, *Sexual Misconduct of the Middle Classes*, and *This is War*, and she has been honoured with numerous awards, among them the Governor General's Literary Award, the Nova Scotia MasterWorks Arts Award, and the prestigious Windham-Campbell Prize. Hannah's music-theatre hybrid *Old Stock: A Refugee Love Story* (co-created with Christian Barry and Ben Caplan) became a *TimeOut* and *New York Times* Critic's Pick, winning both the Herald Angel and a Scotsman Fringe First awards at the Edinburgh Fringe Festival, and receiving six Drama Desk Award nominations in New York, crossing the 400-performance line in the process. In television, Hannah is Co-Creator, Executive Producer, and Head Writer of *Little Bird* alongside showrunner Jennifer Podemski, which has garnered a landslide of awards and critical praise, including the Séries Maria Prix Public (or Audience Award) and thirteen Canadian Screen Awards, including Best Drama Series. Most recently, Hannah was Co-Executive Producer on Season One and Season Two of AMC's hit series *Interview with the Vampire*.